# Fundamentals
# of
# Invitational Education®

## William W. Purkey
*The University of North Carolina at Greensboro*

## John M. Novak
*Brock University*

**The International Alliance for Invitational Education®**
Kennesaw State University
Kennesaw, GA

# CONTENTS

## Table of Contents

# Acknowledgements

We would like to thank the many educators and allied professionals across the world who have brought life to the ideas and adventures of Invitational Education®. You are our heroes, our teachers, and our partners.

A special international thank you is extended to Jennifer Cogswell, from Canada, and Jack Schmidt, from the United States. Together, you artfully showed us that technology can be our friend in making this publication possible. Your editing, polishing, and publishing know-how, along with your tact and patience, have been living examples of Invitational Education in action.

# Preface

For those unfamiliar with Invitational Education®, it is a theory of practice. It is designed to create, maintain, and enhance human environments that cordially summon people to realize their potential in all areas of worthwhile human endeavor. It seeks to explain the nature of "signal systems" that summon forth the realization of human potential, and to identify and change those forces that defeat and destroy potential.

Ideally, the factors of people, places, policies, programs, and processes should be so intentionally inviting as to create a world in which each individual is cordially summoned to develop intellectually, socially, physically, emotionally, and morally.

Increasingly, Invitational Education is finding its way into education at all levels, health care facilities, management in work places, and visionary leadership. It offers concrete, practical, safe, successful, and democratic ways to accomplish its stated mission. It maintains that every person and everything in and around schools and other organizations adds to, or subtracts from, the process of being a beneficial presence in the lives of human beings, personally and professionally. At heart, Invitational Education is an imaginative act of hope.

This booklet begins with an imaginary visit to a public school. However, by applying the fundamentals of Invitational Education presented in this booklet, the visit could just as well have been to a counseling center, general hospital, business office, entertainment facility, and countless other human environments.

# Chapter 1
## *Imagine a Truly Inviting School*

Over the past decade the International Alliance for Invitational Education®, a non-profit organization dedicated to creating, maintaining, and enhancing truly welcoming schools, has presented the *Inviting School Award* to over 150 schools located throughout the United States, South Africa, China (Hong Kong), and Canada. These schools are models for Invitational Education and provide a sample of Invitational Education in action. The following imaginary visit to an Invitational School is based on a composite portrait of these award-winning schools. Many of these practices are found in the book, *Creating Inviting Schools* (Novak, Rocca, & DiBiase, 2006).

A typical question on the minds of an average family relocating to a new geographical location is, "What are the schools like?" Even before the family moves to the new location, the answer begins to reveal itself.

Before moving, the parents subscribe to the local newspaper to look for housing. In the paper, they notice a special column titled, "About Our Schools." They read about a high school choral group who is planning a singing tour of Europe, that two science teachers recently returned from an archeological dig sponsored by the local university, and middle school students have contributed over 2,000 volunteer hours to community service. The article concludes with a list of upcoming school

> *When the parents call the school, the phone is answered promptly and professionally by a friendly human voice.*

events and activities. The large list of sport activities suggests that everyone is encouraged to participate in athletics. It is obvious that the school system has energy, academic purpose, and a commitment to human development in everything it does.

During the move, the family spends considerable time with their realtor, who is a "raving fan" of the local schools. The realtor tells how she recently attended a breakfast reception for the town's realtors hosted by the high school. She was greatly impressed by a group of teachers who presented a brief program on Invitational Education. The program included packets of information and a guided tour of the school. The realtor comments on how the school personnel, including food service personnel, teachers, counselors, librarians, and administrators were courteous, friendly, and professionally dressed.

As the family begins to settle in their new home, they visit the local bank. In the bank foyer is artwork of elementary school students. While visiting a local medical facility, they pick up a copy of the school district newsletter. At the local food store, they read a sign posted by a student organization asking that aluminum cans be saved and dropped off at any local school. The money raised from the sale of cans goes to a relief fund. It is apparent that school programs involve community service and experiences beyond the classroom. That evening the local television news channel reports on the creative academic programs and high student achievement.

The family's next step is to enroll their children in the local public school. When the parents call the school, the phone is answered promptly and professionally by a friendly human voice. The school secretary expresses how happy the school is to enroll their children and makes an appointment for the family to visit the school. The "moment of truth," the family's first impression of the school, is entirely positive.

When the family drives into the school parking lot, they notice that the inviting school philosophy is everywhere, the grass is mowed, bushes trimmed, flowers planted, walkways clean, and the windows sparkle. Although the school was built over fifty years ago, its physical condition conveys the sense of pride that everyone has in the school.

The family comments on the respectful and courteous way signs are worded. Rather than "**No Parking,**" the sign reads, "**Please Park in Designated Areas.**" Instead of "**Visitors Must Report to the Principals' Office,**" the sign reads, "**Welcome to Our School. Please Come to the Principal's Office so We Will Know Who Our Guests Are.**" There are even special parking places marked, "**Reserved for Parents and Adult Caregivers.**" These are signs of things to come.

When the family enters the school, they notice that signs are everywhere, giving directions to the counseling center, cafeteria, restrooms, main office, and welcome center. As they head for the main office, they comment to each other on the living green plants, colorful bright paint, fresh smells, and shining floors. Student work is displayed everywhere.

There is no traditional counter in the main office—only a receptionist's desk and comfortable furniture arranged to make guests feel welcome. The attractive office décor looks more like that of a reception area of a first class corporation, like IBM or Westinghouse, than a traditional public school.

As soon as the family enters the main office, a parent volunteer greets them. The volunteer shakes hands with each family member including the children. She already knows everyone's names and where they are from. The family is then escorted to an attractive room marked "Welcome Center." The center looks like a family living room. There is an array of educational material, a coffee maker, fresh flowers, and ample space to hang coats. The

Welcome Center is the headquarters for many adult volunteers and a reception area for parents and other guests.

Each family member is given personally marked packages of materials, prepared beforehand, describing the school and its invitational philosophy. A student enters the Welcome Center and is introduced by the volunteer. The student will be the family's guide for a school tour.

The student guide explains that she is in the 5$^{th}$ grade and that the school "is the best." She points out that students work cooperatively on academics and discuss with one another during project planning time. Mini courses are available for interested students. Teachers are easy to talk with and are willing to help students with special needs. Grades are assigned in a fair assessment of a student's work and effort.

As the group walks down the hallways, they notice the working clock, water fountains in good repair, up-to-date bulletin boards, and a full-length mirror (for everyone in the school to check their grooming). They enter the school cafeteria, identified by a sign "Dining Room."

The Dining Room has a French village theme. It features scenic murals on the walls, curtains on the windows, individual tables, and even recyclable place mats for student food trays. Family members are surprised that some tables are much higher than others. The guide points out that some students prefer to eat lunch standing up.

*As the group tours the building, they notice that every sign in the school is positively worded.*

Soothing classical music is always played in the cafeteria during lunchtime. "If we can't hear the music, we are being too loud," the student guide explains. A vending machine offers

4

healthy drinks, rather than sodas and colas. Nowhere in the school is there a vending machine with candy, soda, cookies, or chips. It is obvious that the school has an active wellness program in place and that good health practices are encouraged.

One classroom is temporarily unoccupied, so the guide invites the family to take a look. Future student assignments and dates are listed on the board. Student work is displayed on every available wall. The room is clean, orderly, and attractive. It is equipped for the latest electronic teaching technology. Emergency alarm instructions are well posted and easy to follow. One interesting feature is that the students' chairs are padded for comfort, and that the classroom offers a variety of furniture arrangements.

As the group tours the building, they notice that every sign in the school is positively worded. Instead of "**No students allowed!**" on the teachers' workroom door, the sign reads, "**Teachers' Workroom. Please knock before entering. Thank you.**" The guide knocks politely, and then escorts the family in. A large display of educational literature is arranged on ample bookshelves. An attractive up-to-date bulletin board contains information on future academic and social events. Team teaching and interdisciplinary studies are emphasized. Like the rest of the school, the workroom is clean, the air fresh, the furniture comfortable, and the noise subdued.

There are a number of funny, yet friendly, cartoons and clever sayings posted on the workroom bulletin board. Judging by the funny items posted, teachers in this school have a sense of humor and a love of life.

On one wall of the workroom, a large sign reads:

# What is a Student?

**A student is always the most important person in this school ... in person, on the telephone, or by mail.**

**A student is not dependent on us ... we are dependent on the student**

**A student is not an interruption of our work ... the student is the purpose of it.**

**We are not doing a favor by serving the student ... the student is doing us a favor by giving us the opportunity to do so.**

**A student is a human being who brings us his or her desire to learn.**

**It is our job to handle each student in a manner, which is beneficial to the student and ourselves.**

*Adapted from an L.L. Bean Co. poster: "What is a Customer?"*

It is obvious that this teachers' workroom is an important part of an educational institution.

Toward the end of the tour, the family stops off to use the student restrooms. The restrooms are clean and well maintained. Soap and paper-towel dispensers are provided. There is no graffiti. The stalls have doors, and there are mirrors at every sink. Permanent posters remind students to please wash their hands before leaving the restroom.

At the end of the tour the family is escorted to their car and presented with a bumper sticker that reads:

**"Our School: The Most Inviting Place in Town**."

The family begins to understand why this is so.

When the family arrives home and reads the attractive and colorful school information packets, they learn that both the curricular and extracurricular activities call for a high level of student/teacher/parent involvement. School policies reflect unconditional respect for everyone in the school. The principal involves everyone in the decision-making process, and policies are reasonable and enforceable. It is obvious that the school values a democratic ethos.

The next day the family receives a letter from the school thanking them for their visit. They are informed that all paperwork is completed and that the children are officially enrolled. Volunteer groups will soon contact the family. These volunteer groups include band boosters, room sponsors, gardening clubs, athletic boosters, "Senior Active" retired groups, and others who will encourage the family to participate in school life. As the family settles in their new home, there is a wonderful feeling regarding the new school.

Truly inviting schools like the above do exist in growing numbers throughout the United States, Canada, South Africa, Hong Kong, and other countries. These schools do not happen by accident. They are the products of optimism, trust, respect, care, and purpose. The schools are based on regular assessment and a firm commitment to success for everyone. When working with human beings, everything makes a difference, and every accomplishment is significant.

The following chapters will explain the Theory and Practice of Invitational Education, including its foundations. They will also give the basic assumptions of Invitational Education, including

"The Practice," "The Ladder," the "Four Corner Press," the "Stages," and the "Helix."

> *When working with human beings, everything makes a difference, and every accomplishment is significant.*

# Chapter 2
## *Foundations of Invitational Education*

In building a bridge, the structure is of little value without a firm foundation. The key concepts and strategies of Invitational Education are held in place by three interlocking foundations: the democratic ethos, the perceptual tradition, and self-concept theory. Each of these foundations deepens the imaginative possibilities of the inviting approach.

## The Democratic Ethos

Democracy is a social ideal based on the conviction that all people matter and can grow through participation in self-governance. Invitational Education reflects this democratic ethos by emphasizing deliberative dialogue, mutual respect, and the importance of shared activities. The goal of the inviting approach is to have people work together to construct the ethical character, social practices, and educational institutions that promote a fulfilling shared life. Implied here is a respect for people and their abilities to articulate their concerns as they act responsibly on issues that impact their lives. Deeply embedded in this respect for persons is a commitment to the ideal

> *The responsibility of those who adopt Invitational Education as their guide is to summon all involved to develop the perceptions and habits necessary for sustaining such a way of life.*

that people who are affected by decisions should have a say in formulating those decisions.

9

The ideal of democracy is based on a "doing with" as opposed to a "doing to" approach to relating to people. Being "done to" is to be seen as an underling or a vessel to be filled and to be demeaned of inherent dignity and imaginative potential. Being "done with" is to be seen as an active participant in a meaningful process. In addition, participating in democratic practices is vital because it is the deepest way to teach democratic values. Viewed this way, democracy is an educative process, a social way of coming together to enjoy, reflect, and act responsibly. The responsibility of those who adopt Invitational Education as their guide is to summon all involved to develop the perceptions and habits necessary for sustaining a democratic way of life.

## The Perceptual Tradition

The perceptual tradition is based on the assumption that all human behavior is a function of the perceptions that exist for an individual at the moment of acting, particularly those perceptions people hold to be true about themselves and their place in the world.

The word *perception* refers not only to "seeing" but also to "meaning" —the personal significance of an event for the person. The perceptual tradition maintains that all human behavior is a product of how people see themselves and the situations in which they are involved. Although this concept, that people behave according to how they see things, seems obvious, it is often overlooked. The failure of people everywhere to comprehend perception is responsible for much of human misunderstanding, maladjustment, conflict, and loneliness. A critical aspect of Invitational Education is to understand the meaningfulness of people's viewpoints and to work with these perceptions to construct shared purposes.

From a perceptual point of view, there is no such thing as illogical behavior. Each person is doing what makes the most sense to him or her at the moment of acting. No matter how self-defeating, counter-productive, wrong-headed, or apparently stupid a person's behavior appears to be from an external viewpoint, from the individual's internal world, it is the best and safest thing he or she can do right then. Understanding this internal logic helps to explain the dysfunctional actions of many individuals, especially those students who are labeled "at risk," "underachieving," "unmotivated," or "undisciplined." Learning to "read behavior backwards," to see the world from the other person's point of view, is a vital practice for those who wish to apply Invitational Education. We will explore the practice of "reading situations" in more detail in Chapter 7. This practice is deepened by understanding self-concept theory.

## Self-Concept Theory

At the core of each person's perceptual world are the perceptions about oneself. Self-concept is the picture people construct of who they are and how they fit in their perceived world. It is a complex system of personal beliefs that an individual holds to be true about his or her personal existence. It includes all those aspects of the perceptual world to which people refer when they say "I," "me," or even "my" as in the case of *my* gang, *my* country, *my* family, *my* religion, each with a corresponding value. While situations change from moment to moment or place to place, the core beliefs that people hold to be true about themselves are always there as an interpretive basis for determining behavior.

> *A basic assumption of Invitational Education is that there is only one kind of human motivation.*

Like all beliefs, the self-concept resists change. If it changed rapidly, it is difficult to imagine what sort of inconsistent personality a person might have. However, because the self-concept is *learned* through countless interactions with the world, it can be *taught*.

Inside each person there is continuous internal dialogue, this "whispering self" (Purkey, 2002) can be monitored and directed in positive ways. New beliefs develop through life while old ones fade away. A likely explanation for the continuous activity is the assumption that each person constantly strives to maintain, protect, and enhance the perceived self. This assumption is a tremendous and valuable "given" for educators, for it means that the self is predisposed toward realizing its relatively boundless potential in all areas of human activity.

Human motivation is a force that comes from within each person. Rather than spending endless amounts of time trying to "build," "enhance," "shape," "modify," "empower," "turn on," "reward" "reinforce," and "motivate" people, those who apply Invitational Education focus their energies toward finding ways to successfully summon people to see themselves as able, valuable, and responsible and to behave accordingly.

Human motivation is always there. The responsibility of educators is to influence the direction this intrinsic energy and motivation will take. This requires the establishment of "directional road signs," reflecting the basic assumptions of Invitational Education presented in Chapter 3.

> *Human energy and motivation are always there. The role and responsibility of educators is to influence the direction this intrinsic energy and motivation will take.*

# Chapter 3
## *Basic Assumptions of Invitational Education*

Invitational Education is a metaphor for an emerging model of the education process consisting of five value-based assumptions about the nature of people and their potential. It offers a perspective for addressing, evaluating, and modifying the total school environment. This perspective allows the educator to assume an "inviting stance," which is a focused framework for sustained action. This stance consists of five propositions reflecting optimism, trust, respect, care, and intentionality. The dynamic interaction of these propositions is illustrated in Figure 3.1

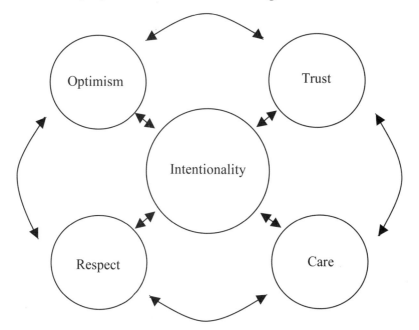

**Figure 3.1 An Inviting Stance**

# Optimism

People possess relatively untapped potential in all areas of positive human endeavor. Challenges, problems, concerns, even "impossibilities" may be invitational opportunities in disguise. Those who practice Invitational Education are committed to the continuous appreciation and growth of all involved in the educative process. They believe that people have only just begun

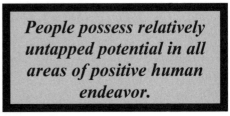

*People possess relatively untapped potential in all areas of positive human endeavor.*

to use their many social, intellectual, emotional, physical, and moral potentials. There are few conditions that humans cannot transcend provided they are suitably invited to do so.

The emphasis on human potential is not a naïve belief that good things will occur automatically. Rather it is a realistic assessment that better things are more likely to occur when self-defeating scripts are held to a minimum. The scripts are described in *What Students Say to Themselves* (Purkey, 2000). The optimism of Invitational Education applies to all realms of possibility, especially in difficult and challenging situations. Even if everything is working against what should and could be done, even the smallest inviting act has the power to make a positive difference.

Human potential, though not always apparent, is always there, waiting to be discovered and invited forth.

# Trust

Invitational Education is a cooperative, collaborative activity. It is built on the fundamental interdependence of human beings. People are viewed as parts of a complex ecosystem whose lives are affected by the quantity and quality of inviting or "disinviting" signal systems sent and received. To develop and sustain a cooperative stance requires the time and effort to establish trustworthy patterns of interaction. Trust is based primarily on the memory of invitations sent, received, and acted upon successfully.

Trustworthy patterns of interaction depend on people who demonstrate the following sources of trust. *Reliability* (consistency, dependability, and predictability), *Genuineness* (authenticity and congruence), *Truthfulness* (honesty, correctness of opinion, and validity of assertions), *Intent* (good character, ethical stance, and integrity), *Competence* (intelligent behavior, expertness), and *Knowledge* (Arceneaux, 1994). Trust is established and maintained through these interlocking human qualities, and each reflects Invitational Education in action.

## Respect

People are valuable, able, and responsible and should be treated accordingly. How educators behave personally and pro-

> *If educators believe that each student is able . . . they will find ways for students to succeed in schools.*

fessionally among themselves and with others is determined by whether they accept this assumption. If educators believe that some students are unable, worthless, and irresponsible, they will find ways to fulfill the prophecy. If educators believe that each student is able to learn, is worthy of respect, and can be responsible, they will find ways for students to succeed in schools.

A democratic society emphasizes the inherent worth of people, believes in their self-directing power, and stresses the importance of personal and social accountability. Invitational schools do the same. They share responsibilities based on mutual respect and expect positive outcomes. This respect is the essence of a cooperative relationship, a relationship that recognizes each person's right to accept, reject, negotiate, or hold in abeyance the messages sent to them, positive or negative. Respect is especially important in inviting positive classroom discipline, as documented by Purkey and Strahan (2002.)

# Care

The process is the product in the making. Means and ends are integrally linked. To attempt to arrive at inviting ends through disinviting means is to disregard how people go about doing anything.

In Invitational Education, care is the ongoing desire to link significant personal means with worthwhile societal ends. This acknowledges the personal need for joy and fulfillment in the process of producing something of value. Careful planning and being oriented to positive possibilities help bring this about.

Of all the propositions that describe Invitational Education, none is more important than the educator's genuine ability and desire to care about others and oneself (Schmidt, 2002). Caring, with its own ingredients, such as warmth, empathy, and positive regard, gives the professional helper the means to be a beneficial presence in one's own life and the lives of other human beings.

> *Of all the propositions that describe Invitational Education, none is more important than the educator's genuine ability and desire to care about others and oneself.*

# Intentionality

Human potential can best be realized by places, policies, programs, and processes specifically designed to encourage development, and by people who are intentionally inviting with themselves and others, personally and professionally. Intentionality is at the very heart of Invitational Education. This fifth assumption of intentionality explains the *how* of Invitational Education. In fundamental practice, Invitational Education focuses on the people, places, policies, and programs that transmit messages promoting human potential.

Invitational Education is characterized by purpose and direction. It recognizes that education can never be neutral and that everything and everybody in and around schools adds to or subtracts from the educative process.

An invitation is never an accident. An invitation is to offer something beneficial for consideration. Thus, an invitation is a choice someone made and a chance someone took.

Assuming an invitational stance provides educators with a shared orientation from which to function. This enables all involved in schools to have a common framework for creating and maintaining a dependably inviting environment. This stance is made evident in the Starfish Analogy, to be explained in Chapter 4.

# Chapter 4
# *The Practice*
# *of Invitational Education*

Invitational Education provides a guiding theory for creating, maintaining, and enhancing truly welcoming schools. Rather than relying on *one* program, *one* policy, *one* place, or *one* process, Invitational Education addresses the total culture or spirit within the school. The goal is to make school a more exciting, satisfying, and enriching experience for everyone—*all* students, *all* staff, and *all* visitors. This effort goes far beyond "restructuring" or "reforming," for its goal is to transform the fundamental culture of the school by centering itself on optimism, trust, respect, care, and intentionality. Invitational Education provides both a language of transformation and a consistent theory of practice.

There are five basic areas that Invitational Education addresses. By focusing on the five powerful "P's that make up every school— people, places, policies, programs, and processes—educators can apply steady and persistent pressure to overcome the biggest challenges. By analogy, this is similar to how a starfish conquers oysters.

## The Starfish Analogy

The starfish lives to eat oysters. To defend itself, the oyster has two stout shells that fit tightly together and are held in place by a powerful muscle. When a starfish locates an oyster, it places itself on the top shell. Then gradually, gently, and continuously, the starfish uses each of its five arms in turn to keep steady pressure on the one oyster muscle. While one arm of the starfish pulls, the others rest. The single oyster muscle, while incredibly powerful, gets no rest. Irresistibly and inevitably, the oyster shell opens and the starfish has its meal. Steady and continuous pressure from a number of points can overcome the biggest muscles of oysters and, by analogy, the biggest challenges faced by any school. Invitational Education requires a wholistic mentality that encompasses *everybody* and *everything* in the school. This is accomplished by paying close attention to the five powerful "P's."

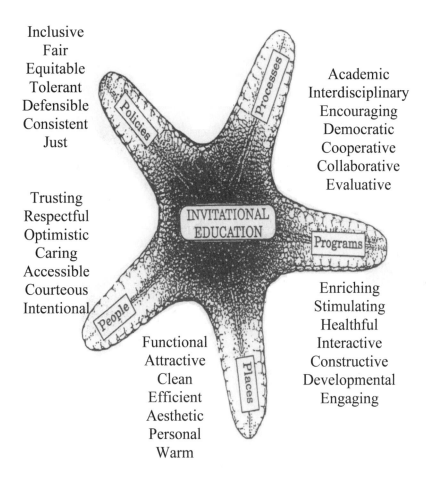

**Figure 4.1 Starfish Analogy**

# People

Invitational Education begins and ends with people. Every person in the school, from teachers and administrators, food service professionals and custodians, counselors and psychologists, librarians and bus drivers, aids and volunteers, and most importantly, students and their adult caregivers, is an emissary of Invitational Education.

Unconditional respect for everyone, intentional caring, and honoring diversity are vital in creating and maintaining inviting schools. Special attention is given to developing a trusting, optimistic, and courteous stance for everyone. Schools that have adopted Invitational Education are easy to spot. They are the ones whose doors are unlocked early on frigid days so that students do not have to stay out in the cold. They are the ones *Invitational Education begins and ends with people.* where the faculty calls students by name, where courtesy and civility are the rule, where staff is accessible, and where there is a general atmosphere of warmth and respect. Places, policies, programs, and processes are all important aspects of Invitational Education, but people come first. If places, policies, programs, and processes directly or indirectly inconvenience people or inhibit their development, these powerful "P's" should be altered.

# Places

Places offer an excellent beginning point for introducing Invitational Education to a school because the physical environment is so visible. If hallways are littered, paint is peeling, restrooms are smelly, classrooms are dusty, offices are cluttered, cafeterias are grimy, grounds are neglected, and windows are dirty, one can assume that the school's policies, programs, processes, and people are the same. From an invitational perspective, there is no excuse for self-induced squalor.

Fortunately, places offer the best opportunity for immediate improvement. Even if the school building is ancient, it is still possible to create a clean, attractive, and inviting physical environment. The landscape and upkeep of the school can announce that people in the school care and are on top of any situation, or they can proclaim that nobody cares and no one feels responsible. This requires careful attention to the aesthetic, clean, functional, and efficient qualities of the school.

## Policies

Policies include official mission statements and the directives, codes, and rules, written and unwritten, used to regulate the schools. A school system's policies can have a strong influence on the attitudes of those involved in the school. When policies are perceived as fair, inclusive, democratic, caring, and respectful, they will have a positive effect on peoples' attitudes.

It is especially important that inviting policies be developed regarding attendance, grading, discipline, and promotion and, as documented by Edwards (2007), the school culture. Above all, they should be fairly applied and reasonably enforced. Policies are critical "semantic webs" that influence the deep-seated structure of any school. All policies are measured by the litmus test question of Invitational Education: Do they reflect optimism, trust, respect, care, and intentionality for everyone in the school?

> *Policies are critical "semantic webs" that inlfuence the deep-seated structure of any school.*

22

## Programs

Programs can be formal or informal, curricular or extra-curricular. It is important for educators to ensure that all the school's programs work for the benefit of everyone and that they encourage active engagement with significant content. This means that programs that appear to be elitist, sexist, ethnocentric, homophobic, discriminatory, or lacking in intellectual integrity need to be changed or eliminated.

In Invitational Education, programs are introduced that emphasize conflict management and group guidance activities. The goal of Invitational Education is to promote and maintain school safety by preventing conflicts before they occur. Programs that reflect Invitational Education are inclusive. They encourage students to see themselves as lifelong learners capable of understanding matters of importance. The use of small-group programs can be especially helpful to enable students to extend their interests and work with others.

## Processes

Finally, a democratic ethos, collaborative and cooperative procedures, and continuous networking among teachers, students, staff, parents, and the community should characterize the processes that give life to a school. In schools where isolation, alienation, and bullying exist, the processes are major contributors. When distilled, processes define the culture of a school, that is, "the way we do things here."

"Processes" address the feel and flavor of the other four qualities and orchestrates them in a democratic manner. Invitational Education is a democratic process in which those who are affected by a decision have a say in its formulation, implementation, and evaluation.

The five powerful P's provide a framework and language for transforming the total school environment. With Invitational Education, everything is connected. This connection might be analogized by thinking of the school as a big bowl of Jell-O: If it is touched anywhere, the whole thing jiggles. Everybody and everything in and around schools adds to or subtracts from the school environment. Thinking about People, Places, Policies, Programs and Processes, each within a framework of respect, trust, optimism, care, and intentionality, provides a strategy for systematic transformation of the whole school.

# Chapter 5
## *The Ladder*

There are many ways to categorize the signal systems found in every school. They can be positive or negative, intentional or unintentional, beneficial or lethal, strong or weak, active or passive, valuable or worthless. They can call people to realize their potential or used to hinder, shun, and destroy people. Often, people are more disinvited than they are disinterested, disadvantaged, disabled, or undisciplined.

The approach in Invitational Education, called the "Ladder," involves the following four categories: *Level One,* intentionally disinviting; *Level Two,* unintentionally disinviting; *Level Three,* unintentionally inviting; and *Level Four,* intentionally inviting.

Earlier the idea was presented that each professional has the ability and responsibility to function in a professionally inviting manner. However, it is possible for a message, no matter how high-minded and well meaning, to be perceived as disinviting. Appealing or repellent qualities remain in the eyes of the beholder. There is no guarantee that the most well-intentioned actions will be viewed positively by others. For example, a person can be seen as rude by being overly polite. The level of a message does not depend solely on what educators do, but on how, when, and why they do it, and ultimately how others perceive their behavior.

Every person and every school occasionally send messages in each of the four levels. However, it is the customary level of functioning that indicates the person's and the school's atmosphere and stance. A dependable stance, where school personnel understand the dynamics of an inviting relationship, increases the likelihood that a cordial summons will be accepted and acted upon. It requires persistence, resourcefulness, and integrity to reach the highest level.

What follows is a four-level "Ladder" for describing what takes place in and around schools. Obviously, the mix of people, places, policies, programs, and processes is much more complex than this simple category. But these four levels provide a starting point for analysis and prescription.

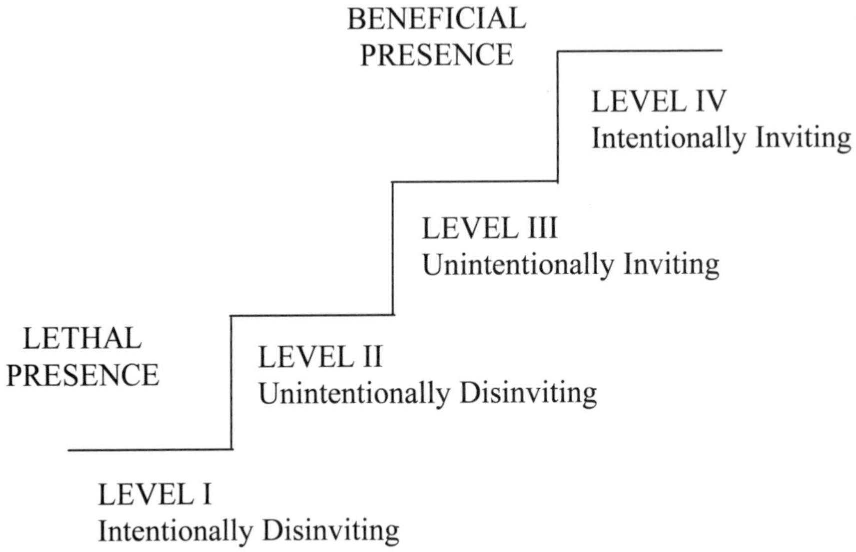

BENEFICIAL
PRESENCE

LEVEL IV
Intentionally Inviting

LEVEL III
Unintentionally Inviting

LETHAL
PRESENCE

LEVEL II
Unintentionally Disinviting

LEVEL I
Intentionally Disinviting

**Figure 5.1    The Ladder – Levels of Professional Functioning**

## Level One: Intentionally Disinviting

This lowest level of functioning describes behaviors, policies, programs, places, and processes that are deliberately designed to demean, diminish, or devalue the human spirit. People who function at this lowest level often use their power to inform others (and themselves) that they are incapable, worthless, and irresponsible.

This bottom level of behavior can be seen in educators who are willfully racist, sexist, homophobic, or elitist. It can be seen in policies that deliberately discriminate or inflict physical pain, such as corporal punishment; programs that are purposefully demeaning,

> *The authors of this book can think of no circumstances in which it is good to demean students.*

such as boot camps; or places, such as bathrooms, that are intentionally left dark and dingy.

A major problem with *Level One* behavior is that these intentionally disinviting actions tend to be justified by the individual and others as being "good" for students. The authors of this book can think of no circumstances in which it is good to demean students or where a professional can justify intentionally disinviting people, places, programs, policies, and processes.

Why a small number of people choose to function at this bottom level is unclear. But regardless of the reasons—whether because of racial, gender, religious, or sexual prejudice, unrequited love, personal inadequacy, or negative self-image—if they are unable or unwilling to change, fellow professionals have the responsibility to caringly remove them from daily contact with students. Intentionally disinviting forces can be lethal to the human spirit.

## Level Two. Unintentionally Disinviting

Intentionally disinviting forces in schools are rare. A much larger concern in schools stems from the people, places, policies, programs, and processes that are unintentionally disinviting. Educators who function at *Level Two* are typically well meaning.

However, by their behavior they inadvertently create and maintain an image that is seen by others as chauvinistic, racist, sexist, homophobic, condescending, or simply thoughtless.

Teachers who are functioning at *Level Two* may not be reflecting on what they are doing. Their classrooms are often characterized by boredom, busywork, and lack of organization. Much of the work students are doing may be seen as irrelevant or incomprehensible and a waste of time.

Schools that operate at *Level Two* are likely to have high dropout and absentee rates for both students and teachers. Morale is low in such schools. Reform strategies are unimaginative or out of touch with the realities the students face.

Educators who function at *Level Two* spend a lot of time wondering, "What did I do wrong?" "Why aren't my students learning more?" "Why do we have such a large turnover of faculty and staff?" "Why is our dropout rate so high?" "Why is everyone so upset with me?" The result is that, in frustration, they often resort to the lowest level, intentionally disinviting functioning.

## Level Three: Unintentionally Inviting

Educators who function at *Level Three* seem to have developed particular ways of functioning that are usually effective, but they have a difficult time explaining why this is so. As successful as they usually are, they lack a consistent stance from which to function. Many so-called "natural born" teachers, those who have never spent much time thinking about why they are successful, are effective because they are functioning at *Level Three*. They typically behave in ways that result in student success, although the teachers are largely unaware of the invitational dynamics involved.

As explained in an earlier book *Inviting School Success: A Self Concept Approach to Teaching and Learning and Democratic Practice* (Purkey & Novak, 1996), professionals who function at *Level Three* are like the early "barn storming" airplane pilots. These pioneer pilots did not know much about aerodynamics, weather forecasts, or navigational systems. It is said that they flew "by the seat of their pants." As long as the weather was kind and they stayed close to the ground so they could follow railroad tracks, they did fine. However, when the weather turned ugly, or night fell, it was easy for them to become disoriented and lost. In other words, they lacked a dependable guidance system.

The difficulty with *Level Three* functioning is that educators can become disoriented. Because they are unable to explain the reasons for their successes, they are unable to explain their failures. If whatever "it" is that accounts for their success stops working, the teachers do not know how to start it up again.

A colleague remarked that he would rather work with someone who is at *Level One* than one who is at *Level Three*. With *Level One* individuals, one knows where he or she stands. With *Level Three*, there is guesswork and unpredictability. Consistency and dependability in education require an intentionally inviting stance.

## Level Four: Intentionally Inviting.

Educators who are intentionally inviting demonstrate integrity in their actions, in the policies and programs they establish, and the places and processes they create and maintain. Because they know *why* they are doing *what* they are doing, *Level Four* educators are able to examine and modify their practices and to grow continuously.

Returning to the barn storming pilot analogy, educators functioning at *Level Four* are like modern commercial jet pilots. Thanks to their knowledge of why things work, they can "fly on instruments" around or over dangerous weather fronts. They have a dependable and identifiable system of navigation.

A deep commitment to *Level Four* functioning is not easy to attain and sustain. It involves a persistence of purpose, an imaginative resourcefulness, and the courage to hold on when the going gets tough. Almost anyone can be inviting when everything is going well and the sun is shining. The real test in Invitational Education is to be inviting when things are going badly, to be "inviting in the rain."

At the intentionally inviting level, educators deliberately choose caring and democratic purposes. They remind themselves of what is truly important in education, an appreciation of people and the value of their development. Those who practice Invitational Education strive to be intentionally inviting in everything they do and in every way they do it. They develop the courage to stand up to cynics and hostile critics because they possess a defensible and self-correcting theory of practice. They prefer to live with their reflected optimism rather than with the self-defeating doubts of others.

> ***Consistency and dependability in education require an intentionally inviting stance.***

# Chapter 6
## *The Four Corner Press*

By its nature, Invitational Education seeks to encourage educators to enrich their lives in four vital corners of one's life: Being personally inviting with themselves; Being personally inviting with others; Being professionally inviting with themselves; and Being professionally inviting with others. The term "Four Corner Press," first presented by Purkey and Siegel in 2003, is used to call attention to the importance of each of the four corners of one's life. The relationship among the Four Corners is illustrated in Figure 6.1.

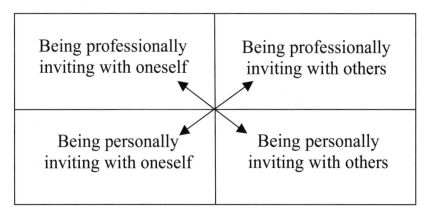

**Figure 6.1    Four Corner Press**

Like a symphony orchestra with its strings, woodwinds, brass, and percussion sections, each corner of the Four Corner Press can be orchestrated to construct a fulfilling, more enriching life, personally and professionally. While there are times when one of the four corners may be temporarily more important and thus receive extra attention, the goal of Invitational Education is to seek balance, harmony, and vibrancy among the four corners. Somewhat like a four-cylinder engine, the four corners require regular fine-tuning to be sure they work in concert.

While the following corners are easy to describe, they are not easy to implement. The challenge is to balance the constant demands of the four corners and artfully blend them together.

> *The challenge is to balance the constant demands of the four corners and artfully blend them together.*

## Corner One:
## Being Personally Inviting with Oneself

To be a long-term beneficial presence in the lives of others, it is vital that educators care for themselves. This means that they view themselves as able, valuable, responsible, and growing in their experiences. Educators who adopt Invitational Education as their theory of practice understand that, while they are not all they could be, they are more than they were, and they like the direction in which they are heading.

An important way to be inviting with oneself is to monitor what one says to oneself internally. Call it mediation, inner conversation, internal dialogue, or self-talk—it is clear that this "whispering self" of inner speech plays a vital role in determining how educators see themselves and how they fit into the world. The importance of the inner voice is documented by Meichenbaum, (1985), Zastrow (1994), Purkey (2000), and many others. Educators who attend to the quality and subtlety of their personal "whispering self," and change the negative to positive interpretations, can enrich their own lives and develop a deeper appreciation of the inner world of others.

## Corner Two:
## Being Personally Inviting with Others

The second important corner of Invitational Education is being personally inviting with others. Most human activities involve interdependence, particularly with family, friends, and co-workers. Invitational Education, with its basic assumptions of optimism, trust, respect, care, and intentionality, points the way to be personally inviting with others.

It is important to remember that all the professional success in the universe will not make up for lack of success with significant others. To promote positive success with family, friends, colleagues, and others, educators are encouraged to develop and maintain care and respect for, and trust in, other human beings. This is especially true when it comes to relationships with students.

Students are keenly aware of the nuances in messages they receive in schools. In Invitational Education, teachers give careful consideration to students' feelings and interests. Making a special effort to learn students' names and interests, sharing out-of-class experiences, and expressing pleasure when the class has performed well are ways that teachers can influence how students perceive themselves as learners and how they perform academically in the classroom.

## Corner Three:
## Being Professionally Inviting
## with Oneself.

It is difficult to overestimate the importance of being active in one's own professional development. The educator who does not invite himself or herself to grow professionally runs the grave risk of becoming obsolete.

Educators, as intellectual workers, have a special responsibility to study the ideas they teach. In a post-modern, pluralistic, democratic culture it is vital that educators attend to the perceptual worlds that students and colleagues bring to the educational setting.

Moreover, educators have a special obligation to gain skill in and be aware of the possibilities and limitations of new electronic sources of information (DiPetta, Novak, & Marini, 2002). The knowledge revolution requires the skill and wisdom of educators who are professionally inviting with themselves.

In practical terms, inviting oneself professionally involves joining professional groups, trying new teaching and counseling methods, participating in online discussion groups, doing research, making professional presentations, spending time reading and writing, and being an active member and leader of a learning community. If a teacher is bored, it is a safe bet that the teacher is boring.

## Corner Four: Being Professionally Inviting with Others

Being professionally inviting with others is best accomplished by building on the strengths provided by the first three corners. Once the first three corners are functioning smoothly, they serve as a means of balance for the fourth corner.

As advocated in previous chapters, the primary purpose of education is to summon people cordially to realize their potential in all areas of worthwhile human activity. This includes meeting the democratic goals of society and participating in the progress of civilization.

Practical strategies for inviting others professionally are so numerous that they have been compiled in a separate book, *The*

*Inviting School Treasury: 1001 Ways to Invite Student Success* (Purkey & Stanley, 2002). The *Treasury* is a desk reference that provides more than a thousand concrete suggestions to improve student academic achievement. None of these suggestions involves bribes, tricks, coercion, or deceptions. This and other helpful books may be ordered through the Radford University Center for Invitational Education, PO Box 7009, Radford University, Radford, VA 24141.

In this chapter, four basic corners of functioning were presented. The successful educator is one who artfully blends and synchronizes the four corners into a seamless whole. The next chapter, Chapter 7, provides a framework of stages involved in creating, maintaining, and enhancing truly inviting relationships and cultures.

> *To be a long-term beneficial presence in the lives of others, it is vital that educators care for themselves.*

# Chapter 7
## *The Stages*

A number of educational, psychological and counseling models have presented stages. These range from human growth and development stages to stages in facing and accepting death. Professional counselors in particular have offered stages in the helping process (Brammer, 1988; Egan, 1994; Ivey & Simek-Downing, 1980, Purkey & Schmidt, 1996). These stages of professional helping usually involve an initial facilitation/introductory stage, a transition stage, and a decision-making stage. Invitational Education follows this pattern in that it proposes a preparation stage, an interaction stage, and a follow-up stage, each with its own components. A more detailed explanation is provided by Schmidt, (2002). The purpose of the following stages is to highlight the basic structure of the inviting process. At the same time, these stages represent a way to look at the complete sequence. As noted earlier in this book, *inviting* is a dynamic and ethical way of "doing-with" other people. Each stage reflects the trust, respect, intentionality, optimism, and care necessary to creatively call forth human potential.

## Preparation Stage

This initial stage consists of having the desire, expecting good things, preparing the setting, and reading situations. All of these factors work in concert.

### Having the desire

It seems obvious that an intentional inclination to be of human service is fundamental to Invitational Education. Wanting to be a beneficial presence in human existence is the foundation of all that follows. However, one caveat is necessary to prevent misinterpretation. It is essential that the desire to help be consistently filtered through the level of one's professional expertise and the welfare of those who are invited.

## Expecting good things

A large number of research studies of professional helpers, including Combs, Avila & Purkey (1978), and Bandura (1986, 1994), has focused squarely on the perceptions of professional helpers. Much of this research has investigated how these perceptual organizations influence effectiveness in helping others. How professional helpers perceive themselves, others, and the situations they face heavily influences their success or failure, personally and professionally. An optimistic view of expecting good things is vital in the inviting process.

## Preparing the setting

Although having the desire and expecting good things are essential, it is equally important to make the total environment to be as welcoming as possible. Within the five powerful "P's" described in Chapter 4, making the "Place" a facilitative physical environment is vital. Professional helpers who take the time to prepare the setting have a head start in developing a truly inviting environment. This includes such everyday policies as scheduling meetings at appropriate times, having materials prepared beforehand, and creating a comfortable environment.

## Reading the situation

Often called sensitivity, empathy, interpersonal perceptivity, and social intelligence, reading situations is the ability to understand what others are feeling and what they are likely to do upon receiving new messages to change behaviors, learn new information, or generally improve their lives. To be successful, an invitation must be both caring and appropriate to the situation. There is a fine line between a compliment and an insult.

Reading situations involves such skills as listening, attending, clarifying, and reflecting. These valuable counseling skills can be learned, and are useful in all types of personal and professional relationships.

## Interacting Stage

This second stage in the inviting process involves choosing carefully among possible options, behaving appropriately, ensuring reception, and honoring the net.

### Choosing carefully

Those who wish to apply Invitational Education as a guiding theory of practice are aware that an opportunity is most likely to be accepted and acted on successfully when four factors are present: (1) the invitation seems safe to accept; (2) there are repeated opportunities to accept; (3) the invitation is clear and unambiguous, and (4) the invitation is not too demanding in intensity and duration. All of these factors are influenced by the inviter.

### Acting appropriately

Choosing with care requires skill and feeling, but the proof is in acting appropriately. Individuals often have good intentions but fail to act on them. Good intentions are of little value unless the inviter acts appropriately. Sometimes, an indirect invitation is less demanding or threatening and is more likely to be accepted and acted upon. As early as 1960, Lippitt and White demonstrated that "guiding suggestions" are characteristics of a democratic relationship: "Have you considered...? " What else could you have done...?" "What is most important to you...? The major characteristic on each of these guiding suggestions is respect for people and their self-directing powers.

## Ensuring reception

Everyday, people send inviting messages that are never received. Notes are misfiled, phone messages are misplaced, emails get erased, and comments go unheard. Because messages can be misdirected, misplaced, or misunderstood, it is vital to insure that the content of a message is received and acknowledged. Ensuring reception is clearly the responsibility of the sender.

## Honoring the net

In the game of tennis, going over the net is a "fault." The "net" in Invitational Education is a hypothetical boundary between the sender and the receiver that marks the inviolable territory for each party, a concept created by Stafford (2003) in his application of Invitational Education to the practice of professional counseling.

There is a certain etiquette involved in Invitational Education. No matter how much the sender wants the invitation to be accepted, and no matter how beneficial the invitation might be, the receiver maintains the absolute right to decide what to do with it. Otherwise, the invitation would be nothing more than sugarcoated coercion.

# Follow-up Stage

In the follow-up stage, inviting processes include interpreting responses, negotiating positions, evaluating the process and progress, and reinforcing trust.

## Interpreting responses

When a professional helper sends an invitation and it is received, it becomes the property of the receiver. The receiver has the options of accepting, not accepting, ignoring it, modifying it with a counter proposal, or tabling it until another time. What is critical is the sender's interpretation of the receiver's response. Non-acceptance does not necessarily mean rejection. Sometimes, people who are invited wait for the invitation to be repeated more than once or twice. This is done to ensure that the sender is sincere and the invitation is valid.

## Negotiating

Those who apply Invitational Education seek to address challenges and manage difficulties by working around them. Using Invitational Education to negotiate challenges is described by Purkey and Strahan in their book, *Inviting Positive Classroom Discipline* (2002). Chapter 6 of Purkey and Strahan's book is devoted to a detailed explanation of the invitational approach to conflict management.

## Evaluating the process and progress

Formal or informal evaluation is unavoidable in any human endeavor. Assessment is an important tool of professional helpers. To provide optimal service, professional helpers use a wide range of instruments and techniques. In schools, standardized tests and inventories are used to help students achieve success. In clinics, professionals use observations, interviews, and surveys to assist clients. In hospitals, medical personnel use the latest of scientific equipment to help heal patients. Regardless of the type of evaluation, whether informal or formal procedures are used, it is essential that continuous evaluation on process and progress takes place.

## Reinforcing trust

Trust is so vital to Invitational Education that it is presented in Chapter 3 as one of its five basic assumptions. Trust is greatly influenced by experiences. Without a reasonable amount of trust, people will not self-disclose, explore new ideas and opportunities, or take the risks necessary to find new ways of being.

Invitational Education is a cyclical process. Just as the helix (to be described in the next chapter) flows upward, one sequence leads to another. Trust develops as a result of successive levels of positive and beneficial experiences. While the three stages outlined here are highlighted for the sake of analysis, it is necessary to state again that Invitational Education consists simultaneously of many separate activities, with many overlapping and seamless components. In this sense, Invitational Education may be viewed as an overarching summons for people to realize their relatively boundless potential in all areas of their lives. The inviting stages described briefly in this chapter lend intimacy to all educational, clinical, and other helping relationships. Attention to each step is a way to examine what went right or wrong, and what else might be done to encourage movement in a given relationship. By recognizing and using the stages and their respective components, professionals are able to pinpoint and adjust their beliefs and behaviors, and thereby provide dependable assistance to those they serve.

The final chapter will explain the "Helix." The Helix demonstrates how educators can move from awareness, to understanding, to application, to adoption of Invitational Education.

# Chapter 8
## *The Helix*

The "Helix" is defined as something spiral in form. The term seems to fit the developmental nature of Invitational Education. Beginning with initial exposure to the theory, educators can spiral upward from occasional interest, to systematic application, to pervasive adoption. The Helix is based on the idea that for educators to involve themselves in Invitational Education, they spiral upward from being aware of it, to understanding it, to applying it, and finally adopting it as a pervasive theory of practice. Attempting to jump directly from awareness to adoption without going through the Helix process is unlikely to be successful.

Commitment to Invitational Education may vary in intensity. Some schools may be seeking to introduce a few inviting practices, others may be wishing to apply it systematically, while still others may be wanting to use Invitational Education as a pervasive philosophy to guide everything involved in the educative process. But whatever the intensity, it is important to remember that even the smallest inviting act is significant. To an emotionally starving person, the smallest invitation can be a feast.

Using the four upward spiraling stages of **awareness, understanding, application**, and **adoption**, and three phases of interest from **occasional**, to **systematic**, to **pervasive**, the Helix provides a 12-step guide to school trans-formation. Figure 8.1 illustrates the Helix.

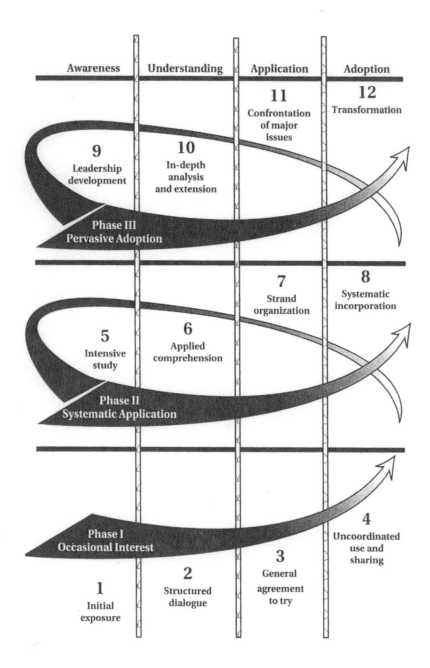

**Figure 8.1    The Helix**

# Occasional Interest (Phase I)

A key foundation of Invitational Education is to build on the good things that are already being done in the school. During this initial phase, generous recognition and praise are given to a variety of good practices already in place. This is followed by descriptions of what other schools are doing that the school might want to try. The purpose is to create awareness of, and to introduce, Invitational Education.

**Step 1. Initial Exposure.** Beginning awareness of Invitational Education can happen by talking to a colleague, reading some introductory materials, such as this booklet, hearing a speaker, watching a video, or PowerPoint, or attending a conference. Initial exposure should be an enjoyable experience. It should remind educators of the nobility of teaching and what really matters in education.

**Step 2. Structured Dialogue.** This step involves organized discussion following a program, speech, meeting, or reading of materials. Emphasis is on recognizing and appreciating inviting practices already taking place. Exploring *why* these practices are inviting is a valuable activity.

**Step 3. General Agreement to Try.** The purpose here is to seek a consensus to test out a variety of new ideas, see what works, and what might be continued. This step involves small alterations, such as changing the wording of signs on and in a school, adding additional lighting, cleaning up the trash disposal area, or starting a new extracurricular club. These changes may be considered temporary and can serve as a preliminary test of Invitational Education. By labeling the changes "temporary," it consoles those who typically resist change.

**Step 4. Uncoordinated Use and Sharing.** During this step individuals and groups report on what changes went well, what could be improved, and how the improvement might be accomplished. Many of the new initiatives are adopted and are publicly recognized. As examples, telephone calls to the school are handled promptly, politely, and efficiently, and all visitors to the school receive immediate and cordial recognition. Highlighting successful new practices sets the stage to spiral upward toward deeper levels of Invitational Education.

## Systematic Application (Phase II)

After a period of initial small successes, groups can work to introduce integrative change within the school. Integrative change means that people are willing to work together and look beyond their subject matter and classrooms to find ways to make the whole school a shared concern.

**Step 5: Intensive Study.** An awareness of Invitational Education as a positive systemic approach is introduced here. Invitational Education, with its foundations, assumptions, practices, levels, four corners, and Helix are presented by an experienced leader in the school or by an Invitational Education consultant. Ideally this leader has a solid background of knowledge of Invitational Education and demonstrates it in his or her personal and professional life.

**Step 6: Applied Comprehension.** Comprehension means that those involved make Invitational Education an integrated plan based on the five P's presented in Chapter 4. Those involved take the time to share their understanding of Invitational Education's key ideas. It is here that what is currently happening in the school is examined in terms of the assumptions of optimism, trust, respect, care, and intentionality, and the rigorous criteria of the 5-'Ps for being an inviting school.

**Step 7: Strand Organization.** Using the 5-P's of Invitational Education presented in *Chapter 4*, teams of strands are organized whose members are representative of the entire school family, including custodians, food service professionals, counselors, librarians, administrators, psychologists, students, and adult caregivers. These individuals are randomly assigned into five groups: People, Places, Policies, Programs, and Processes called "Strands." Each Strand focuses on its particular "P."

As strands woven together make a rope, Strands in schools woven together create Invitational Education. At intervals, each Strand shares its invitational goals with the entire school, along with its ways of proceeding, obstacles envisioned, ways to overcome obstacles, and methods of evaluation. Each Strand selects its own chairperson.

Invitational goals are established by a creative consensus of Strand members.

**Step 8: Systematic Incorporation.** It is now time for each of the five Strands to establish its own identity. The Strand members meet regularly. In addition, Strand chairs also meet together on a regular basis. Information regarding progress is given to all members of the school community. During this step, networks may be formed with other inviting schools.

## Pervasive Adoption (Phase III)

In this highest phase of the Helix, Invitational Education permeates the school and becomes the way in which everything is done. School personnel move outside the school and begin to provide leadership to other schools and systems. In doing so, school personnel strengthen their own bonds with Invitational Education.

**Step 9: Leadership Development.** An appreciation of the complexity of Invitational Education develops as emerging leaders formally explore the relationship between Invitational Education and other school goals. Members of the 5-P Strands consider ways to explore new ways of teaching, leading, and living.

**Step 10: Depth Analysis and Extension.** A deep understanding of Invitational Education means that educators critically analyze it and compare and contrast it with other approaches. An even deeper understanding is demonstrated by the ability to translate other approaches into acceptable or unacceptable practices from an inviting perspective. New program initiatives are examined and modified using the criteria involved in Invitational Education.

**Step 11: Confrontation of Major Concerns.** At this point, members of the school community take a proactive stance and address key issues that affect the school and community. Many of these key issues, such as racism, sexism, elitism, favoritism, and the nature of privilege have long been taboo subjects. Insights and participation from students, parents, faculty, staff, parents, and others outside the school are used to develop a deep sense of purpose for the school.

**Step 12: Transformation.** At this highest point in the Helix, Invitational Education permeates the whole school. The school functions somewhat like an inviting family. There is optimism, respect, trust, care, and an invitational intentionality everywhere in and around the school. The school serves as a model for what

> *The aim is to realize human potential through sustained imaginative acts of hope.*

schools can become, and members of the school community make presentations at other schools and conferences. Celebrations of success are everywhere.

For a list of Inviting Schools, and details on the **Inviting School Award**, please contact The International Alliance for

Invitational Education at Kennesaw State University, Marietta Georgia.

## Conclusion

After a long period of being in an educational dark age of high stakes testing, zero tolerance, mandatory retention, aggressive discipline, and negative labeling of students, teachers, and schools, a renaissance is in sight. Invitational Education is one voice in this renaissance. The aim is to realize human potential through sustained imaginative acts of hope.

*Fundamentals of Invitational Education* describes the basics of Invitational Education and provides the foundations, assumptions, practices, levels, the four corners, and the Helix of invitational theory of practice. This booklet hopes to give a clearer articulation of this larger global education movement so that it can gain strength throughout the world.

Already, the International Alliance for Invitational Education®, a not-for-profit tax-exempt organization, has established itself in Hong Kong, South Africa, Canada, and throughout the United States. *The Alliance is the only non-profit organization in existence whose primary mission is to create, maintain, and enhance truly welcoming schools.* The reader is cordially summoned to join the Alliance and provide invitational leadership for the decades to come. Contact the International Alliance for Invitational Education® Headquarters at Kennesaw State University or visit the website at www.invitationaleducation.net for details on how to be a participant and help make our world a more optimistic, trusting, respecting, caring and intentionally inviting place for everyone.

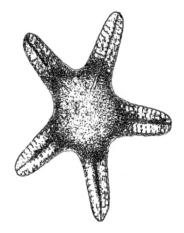

# References and Resources

Amos, L. (1985) *Professionally and personally inviting teacher practices as related to affective course outcomes reported by dental hygiene students.* Doctoral dissertation, The University of North Carolina at Greensboro.

Asbill, K. (2000). *Invitational leadership: Teacher perceptions of inviting principal practices.* Doctoral dissertation, New Mexico State University.

Asbill, K., & Gonzalez, M. (2001). Invitational leadership: Teacher perceptions of inviting principal practices. *Journal of Invitational Theory and Practice, 7,* 12-15.

Arceneaux, C.J. (1994). Trust: An exploration of its nature and significance. *Journal of Invitational Theory and Practice. 3,* 5-49.

Bandura, A. (1986). *Social foundations of thought and action: A social cognitive theory.* Englewood Cliffs, NJ: Prentice Hall.

Bandura, A. (1994). Self-efficacy. In V.S. Ramachaudram (Ed.) *Encyclopedia of human behavior.* (Vol. 4, pp 71-81). New York: Academic Press.

Brammer, L. M. (1988). *The helping relationship: Process and skills (4th Ed).* Englewood Cliffs, NJ: Prentice Hall.

Combs, A. W., Avila, D. L. & Purkey, W. W. (1978). *Helping relationships: Basic concepts for the helping profession.* (2nd ed.) Boston: Allyn & Bacon.

DiPetta, T., Novak, J., & Marini. Z. (2002). *Inviting online education.* Bloomington, IN: Phi Delta Kappa.

DuFour, R., & Eaker, R. (1998). *Professional learning communities at work: Best practices for enhancing student achievement.* Bloomington, IN. National Educational Service.

Egan, G. (1994). *The skilled helper: A model for systematic helping and interpersonal relating* (5th ed.). Pacific Grove, CA: Brooks/Cole.

Edwards, W. (2007) Policy matters at the school level. *National Dropout Prevention Newsletter, 19*(2), Spring 2007.

Egley, R. (2003). Invitational leadership: Does it make a difference? *Journal of Invitational Theory and Practice, 9,* 57-70.

Harper, K. & Purkey, W.W. (1993). Self-concept-as learner of middle level students. *Research in Middle Level Education, 17*(1), 80-89.

Ivey A. E. & Simek-Downing, L. (1980). *Counseling and psychotherapy: Skills, theory and practice.* Englewood Cliffs, NJ: Prentice-Hall.

Lippitt, R. & White, R. (1960). *Autocracy and democracy.* New York: Harper & Row.

Lueder, D. (1989). Tennessee parents were invited to participate and they did. *Educational Leadership, 47,* 15-17.

Meichenbaum, D. (1985). *Stress inoculation training.* New York: Pergamon.

Novak, J.M. Ed. (1992). *Advancing invitational thinking.* San Francisco: Caddo Gap Press.

Novak, J.M. (1999). Inviting criteria for democracy's schools. *Thresholds in Education. 25*(1), 4-6.

Novak, J.M. (2002). *Inviting educational leadership. Fulfilling potential and applying an ethical perspective to the educational process.* London: Pearson.

Novak, J.M. (2003). Invitational leadership and the pursuit of educational living. (B. Davies & J. West-Burnham Eds.). *Handbook of educational leadership and management.* London: Pearson. 67-74.

Novak, J.M. (2005). Invitational leadership. (B. Davies Ed.). *Essentials of school leadership.* London: Chapman. 44-60.

Novak, J.M. & Purkey, W.W. (2001). *Invitational Education.* Bloomington, IN: Phi Delta Kappa.

Novak, J.M., Rocca, W., and DiBiasi A. (Eds.) (2006). *Creating inviting schools.* San Francisco: Caddo Gap.

Purkey, W.W. (1970*). Self-concept and school achievement.* Englewood Cliffs, NJ: Prentice-Hall.

Purkey, W. W. (2000). *What students say to themselves: Internal dialogue and school success.* Thousand Oaks, CA: Corwin Press.

Purkey, W. W. (2006). *Teaching class clowns: (and what they can teach us).* Thousand Oaks, CA: Corwin Press.

Purkey, W.W., & Novak, J.M. (1996). *Inviting school success: A self-concept approach to teaching, learning, and democratic practice.* (3rd ed.). Belmont CA: Wadsworth.

Purkey, W.W., & Novak, J.M. (1997). An Invitational approach to conflict management. *Thresholds in Education,* 22(4), 24-27.

Purkey, W. W., & Powell, D. (2005). An Invitational approach to overcoming tough challenges. *Tennessee Principal.* Spring. Issue. 25-28.

Purkey, W. W., & Schmidt, J. (1987). *The inviting relationship: An expanded perspective for professional counseling.* Englewood Cliffs, NJ: Prentice Hall.

Purkey, W. W. & Schmidt, J. J. (1996). *Invitational counseling: A self-concept approach professional practice.* Pacific Grove, CA: Brooks/Cole.

Purkey, W. W., & Siegel, B.L. (2003). *Becoming an invitational leader.* Atlanta, GA: Humanics Press.

Purkey, W. W. & Stanley, P. H. (2002). *The inviting school treasury.* Greenville, NC: Brookcliff Publishers.

Purkey, W. W. & Strahan, D. B. (2002). *Inviting positive classroom discipline.* Westerfield, OH: National Middle School Association.

Riner, P. (2003). The intimate correlation of Invitational Education and effective classroom management. *Journal of Invitational Theory and Practice. 9*, 41-55.

Schmidt, J. J. (2002). *Intentional helping: A philosophy for proficient caring relationships.* Upper Saddle River, NJ: Prentice Hall.

Stafford, W. B. (2003). To honor the net in invitational counseling. *Journal of Invitational Theory and Practice, 9,* 9-22.

Stanley, P.H. & Purkey, W.W. (1994). Student self-concept as learner: Does Invitational Education make a difference? *Research in the Schools, l,* 15-27.

Zastrow, C. (1994). Conceptualizing and changing the self from a rational therapy perspective. In T. M. Brinthaupt & R. R\P. Lipka (Eds.). *Changing the self: Philosophies, techniques, and experiences,* (pp. 175-199). Albany, NY: State University of New York Press.

## The International Alliance for Invitational Education®

The International Alliance for Invitational Education® is chartered by the State of North Carolina as a not-for-profit oganization and designated by the IRS as a 501(3)(e) charitable organization. Members consist of an international network of professional educators and helpers who seek to apply the concepts of Invitational Education to their personal and professional lives.

Because International Alliance for Invitational Education is dedicated to democratic principles, its mission is to enhance life-long learning, promote positive change in organizations, cultivate the personal and professional growth and satisfaction of education and allied professionals, and enrich the lives of human beings personally and professionally.

The Alliance office is located at Kennesaw State University, Georgia, U.S.A. The mailing address is:

P. O. Box 5173
Marietta, GA  30061-5173

The Alliance website is: www.invitationaleducation.net

# Index